**REED**

BOOKS BY AI

Cruelty, 1973
Killing Floor, 1979
Sin, 1986
Fate, 1991

GREED

Ai

W. W. Norton & Company   *New York   London*

THE POEMS IN THIS BOOK HAVE APPEARED IN
THE FOLLOWING MAGAZINES:

Agni Review: "Self Defense," Life Story," "Hoover, Edgar J."; *Callaloo:* "Knockout," "Self Defense"; *Caprice:* "Finished," "Appomattox," "Penis Envy"; *Graham House Review:* "Zero Velocity, II"; *Lingo:* "Respect, 1967"; *Muleteeth:* "Jack Ruby on Ice," "Riot Act"; *On the Bus:* "Reconciliation, 2, 3, 4," "Zero Velocity, I," "Self Defense," "Archangel"; *Ploughshares:* "Family Portrait, 1960"; *Snail's Pace Review:* "Oswald Incognito & Astral Travels," "Party Line," *Tribes:* "Miracle in Manila"; *University of Louisville Review:* "Reconciliation, 1"; *Zone:* "The Ice Cream Man."

These dramatic monologues are 100 percent fiction and are merely characters created by the poet. Some of them project the names of "real" public figures onto made-up characters in made-up circumstances. Where the names of corporate, media, or public or political figures are used here, those names are meant only to denote figures, images, the stuff of imagination; they do not denote or pretend to private information about actual persons, living, dead, or otherwise.

The text of this book is composed in Granjon with the display set in Geometric 415 Bold. Composition by PennSet, Inc. Manufacturing by The Courier Companies, Inc. Book design by Guenet Abraham.

Library of Congress Cataloging-in-Publication Data

Ai, 1947–
   Greed / Ai.
     p.   cm.
   1. Avarice—Poetry. I. Title.
   PS3551.I2G74   1993
   811'.54—dc20   93-9920

ISBN 0-393-03561-1

W. W. Norton & Company, Inc.
500 Fifth Avenue New York, N.Y. 10110

W. W. Norton & Company Ltd.
10 Coptic Street London WC1A 1PU

1 2 3 4 5 6 7 8 9 0

This book is dedicated to my loyal fans.

CONTENTS

REED

Riot Act, April 29, 1992

I'm going out and get something.
I don't know what.
I don't care.
Whatever's out there, I'm going to get it.
Look in those shop windows at boxes
and boxes of Reeboks and Nikes
to make me fly through the air
like Michael Jordan
like Magic.
While I'm up there, I see Spike Lee.
Looks like he's flying too
straight through the glass
that separates me
from the virtual reality
I watch everyday on TV.
I know the difference between
what it is and what it isn't.
Just because I can't touch it
doesn't mean it isn't real.
All I have to do is smash the screen,
reach in and take what I want.
Break out of prison.
South Central homey's newly risen
from the night of living dead,
but this time he lives,
he gets to give the zombies
a taste of their own medicine.
Open wide and let me in,
or else I'll set your world on fire,

but you pretend that you don't hear.
You haven't heard the word is coming down
like the hammer of the gun
of this black son, locked out of the big house,
while massa looks out the window and sees only smoke.
Massa doesn't see anything else,
not because he can't,
but because he won't.
He'd rather hear me talking about mo' money,
mo' honeys and gold chains
and see me carrying my favorite things
from looted stores
than admit that underneath my Raiders' cap,
the aftermath is staring back
unblinking through the camera's lens,
courtesy of CNN,
my arms loaded with boxes of shoes
that I will sell at the swap meet
to make a few cents on the declining dollar.
And if I destroy myself
and my neighborhood
"ain't nobody's business, if I do,"
but the police are knocking hard
at my door
and before I can open it,
they break it down
and drag me in the yard.
They take me in to be processed and charged,
to await trial,
while Americans forget
the day the wealth finally trickled down
to the rest of us.

SELF DEFENSE

For Marion Barry

Y'all listen to me.
Why can't I get a witness?
Why can't I testify?
You heard the bitch. You heard her say
I can't even caress her breast.
Unless I smoke for sex,
I get next to nothing.
I get set up for spread thighs.
I am the mayor of Washington, D.C.
and I can be as nasty as I wanta.
You think you can chew me up
and spit me down in the gutter,
but I am there already.
I have no other choice.
I am a victim of the white press,
but I have the antidote for all your poison.
The rock of this age is crack
and like the primal urge to procreate,
desire for it surges through you,
until you praise its name
in the same breath as you do Jesus.
The need seizes addicts and lifts them to heaven
by the scruff of the neck,
then hurls them back,
drops in my lap a slut
who wouldn't even squeeze my nuts
for old times' sake,
but made me puff that substitute,
until you FBI came bursting in.

Now I'm sure you think you should have shot me,
should have pretended I pulled a gun
and to defend yourselves, you had to do it.
You could have been through with it.
I could have been just another statistic.
I *am* realistic.
I am a man condemned for his weakness.
Had I been white,
I would have been the object of sympathy, not ridicule.
Trick me? Convict me?
Now, now you know
I'm not a man you can control.
The good ole days of slaves out pickin' cotton
ain't coming back no more. No,
with one drag, I took my stand against injustice.
Must a man give up his vices
because he is the mayor?
You made me a scapegoat,
one black man against the mistah massa race.
You thought I would cave in
and take my whuppin',
take my place
back of the endless soupline of the nineteen nineties,
as if it were still the fine and white fifties,
where y'all drink tea in the palour
and the colored maids don't get no farther
than the next paycheck,
the next hand-me-downs from Mrs. so and so.
Po' ole mammies, po' ole black Joes,
working for low wages.
You don't need to quote my rights to me.
Don't they stick in your throat? Don't they?
All that marching and riding,

even torching Watts and Cleveland
gave us the right to vote,
but reading rights won't make a difference
if the verdict is already in.
You can't depend on nothing.
You got to toughen yourself.
I paid for my slice of American pie,
but you lie and say I stole it.
That is how you hold the nigger down
and beat him to death with his own freedom.

ENDANGERED SPECIES

The color of violence is black.
Those are the facts, spread-eagled
against a white background,
where policemen have cornered the enemy,
where he shouldn't be, which is seen.
Of course, they can't always believe their eyes,
so they have to rely on instinct,
which tells them I am incapable
of civilized behavior,
therefore, I am guilty
of driving through my own neighborhood
and must take my punishment
must relax and enjoy
like a good boy.
If not, they are prepared to purge me
of my illusions of justice, of truth,
which is indeed elusive,
much like Sasquatch,
whose footprints and shit
are only the physical evidence
of what cannot be proved to exist,
much like me,
the "distinguished" professor of lit,
pulled from my car,
because I look suspicious.
My briefcase, filled with today's assignment,
could contain drugs,
instead of essays arranged
according to quality of content,

not my students' color of skin,
but then who am I to say
that doesn't require a beating too?—
a solution that leaves no confusion
as to who can do whatever he wants to whom,
because there is a line directly
from slave to perpetrator,
to my face staring out of newspapers and TV,
or described over and over as a black male.
I am deprived of my separate identity
and must always be a race instead of a man
going to work in the land of opportunity,
because slavery didn't really disappear.
It simply put on a new mask
and now it feeds off fear
that is mostly justified,
because the suicides of the ghetto
have chosen to take somebody with them
and it may as well be you
passing through fire,
as I'm being taught
that injustice is merely another way
of looking at the truth.
At some point, we will meet
at the tip of the bullet,
the blade, or the whip
as it draws blood,
but only one of us will change,
only one of us will slip
past the captain and crew of this ship
and the other submit to the chains
of a nation
that delivered rhetoric
in exchange for its promises.

HOOVER, EDGAR J.

1

I'm the man behind the man
behind the man
and I have got my hands
in everybody's pockets.
I know who's been sticking his plug
in Marilyn Monroe's socket.
The shock it would give,
if everybody knew what King Arthur Jack
won't do to keep his rocket fueled.
I have files on everyone who counts,
yet they would amount to nothing,
if I did not have the will to use them.
Citizens must know their place,
but so must the President,
who simply decided one day
to hock his family jewels to the Mob.
They call me a cruel sonofabitch
just to aggravate me,
but my strength is truth.
I have the proof
of every kind of infidelity
and that makes me the one free man
in a country of prisoners
of lust, greed, hatred, need
greater than the fear of reprisal,
all the recognized sins
and all those unrecognizable,
except to me and God. Maybe God.

Sometimes my whole body aches
and I lie down on the floor,
just staring at the ceiling,
until I am feeling in control again,
my old confidence surging back
through me like electricity
and I get up, Frankenstein, revived
by the weakness of others
and as unstoppable as a handful of pills
that might kill you on a night like this,
like the night when Marilyn kissed it all goodbye.
It only came up roses after her show closed.
Too bad she had to row, row her boat
in lava lake.
They said they would make her a star.
Now far out in space,
her face big as a planet,
she looks down
on the whole pathetic, human race, wasting time,
as it shivers and shakes
down the conga line
behind Jack, Bobby, and me too.
When the voice on the phone
cried *"We're through"* and hung up,
she took an overdose,
trusting someone to save her,
but now she whispers,
"Honey, don't trust anybody
and never, ever fuck the head of state."

2

I had a head bald
as a licked clean plate
and a face . . .
Nobody ever said grace at my table,
yet, the god of judgment hovered over my head.
He led me down
dark halls to motel rooms,
where a locked door
and heavy perfume
could neither conceal, nor contain
the fumes of love that proclaimed
another fallen angel by his name.
Martin Luther King, Jr. preaches freedom,
but it means slavery for the white man.
It hands our keys to the robbers
and says, please, don't take anything.
Look at him on his knees
before pussy's altar.
Tomorrow with his wife beside him
he won't falter, as he shouts
from the pulpit about equality.
His words are a disease sweeping
through the colored people.
I can stop it if I choose.
I can release the tapes, the photographs
and end the so-called peaceful revolution,
but my solution is to sabotage discreetly,
to let someone else take the blame,
the Klan, or even another smoke,
who's younger and not broken in by privilege.
Someone like that Malcolm X,

that showstopping nigger,
who respects no boundaries
and hates the white man,
because he understands him.
He doesn't want to vote,
he doesn't want to tote that bail
in the name of integration.
He wants to sail back into blackness
and I say let him.
There is no such thing as freedom
and there never will be,
even for the white man.
The X-man knows it is eat, or be eaten
and Grandpa Hoover
has the biggest teeth.

3

They all wanted me
to take the A train to anonymity,
those who would seduce their own mothers,
after an audience with the Pope.
The Holy joke I call him.
I'd like to get a tape, or two,
of that crew in Rome.
A two-way mirror
somewhere in the Vatican, the camera rolling,
while some Cardinal is jerking off
over a silver bowl,
until his Vesuvius erupts again and again.
But I digress.
Now Lyndon Johnson and a negress,
that *is* delicious,

something best served on a platter.
Save it until after the elections
when it really matters.
I'm so scattered lately.
I feel like shattering all my Waterford crystal.
Ask me anything you want, but don't touch me.
I keep my pistol loaded.
Don't say I told you. Do.
I want the lowdown sonsofbitches
who betray me to know
I'm on to them like a fly on shit.
I will not rest,
until I spit in their mouths
and piss on their faces. The fools.
J. Edgar Hoover runs this country.
J. Edgar Hoover rules.

HOOVER TRISMEGISTUS

I rode the tail of a comet into the world.
Whether I were Edgar, or Mary
meant nothing to me.
I could be both, couldn't I?
That part was easy,
but what I couldn't tolerate
was the face in the bathroom mirror.
Was I a throwback to some buck
who sat hunched over in the hull
of a ship,
while the whip lashed his back?
"Do I look colored to you?" I ask Clyde,
who always, always turns aside my question,
as if he already knows the truth,
as if I have the proof in my possession
like a passport to destruction,
but a man who has fear on his side
can do anything.
Any dictator knows that.
You think Castro doesn't know it, or Chairman Mao?
There's a man I secretly admired.
We could have used a cultural revolution here.
Hell, we nearly had one.
The House un-American activities were a start,
but we didn't go far enough.
When they called Joe McCarthy's bluff,
he grabbed his nuts and ran
and the others banned together
to save their asses

anyway they could,
except for good old Roy Cohn,
a man after my own heart,
because he has none.
"Mary," he always tells me,
"what a red dress and high heels won't do
to lift a gal's spirits."
He's right.
When I have another one of my nightmares
of walking through high cotton
to a tree, where the boy swinging
at the end of a rope
opens his mouth and speaks to me,
saying, "One more nigger to go,"
I tell Roy to book that suite at the Plaza.
I know that Mississippi
is a state of mind we all carry in us
like a virus that activates
just when we think we're safe,
so of course, it isn't long
before I find my darker side
at a party up in Harlem.
He comes to me only once,
the love that twice dares not
speak its name.
See my divine black boy, fumbling with his zipper
while I wait impatiently,
hoping someone will see
that I am being had against my will
that I will deny the darkie inside me by killing him.
Still, he rises when he's done with me,
the gunshot wound through his heart

still bleeding profusely,
the knife still protruding from his back.
In other words, he is my destiny.
Afterward, Roy arranges transportation for him,
plus a few dollars.
He tells him to chalk it up
to experience and let it be,
because there is no future in loving me.
I like *that*.
"You hear me, boy?" Roy asks him.
"Yes," he whispers.
"Yes, what?" asks Roy.
"Yes, sir!"
He may as well say, yes, master.
"Ask her," the boy says, meaning me,
"whether or not she is satisfied."
"Please," says Roy, "leave while you still can."
After that, my experiments in degradation
begin in earnest.
How many nights do I fight my desire
by giving in to it
and dreaming about him?
How many times do I pull down his pants
as he now swings from that rope,
only to find bloody holes,
where his genitals should be
and foiled again,
descend into the ship of myself,
where the slaves are jammed in so tightly,
all I can see is a mass of darkness,
not people,
though I can smell them,

though it is nothing compared
to the smell of my own fear,
because it's here I belong,
here on the endless crossing
into whiteness.

JACK RUBY ON ICE

"Shit, I heard they [Ruby and Oswald] were queer for each other."
—*Double Cross*, Sam and Chuck Giancana

A man needs ammunition,
because a bullet at the right time
accomplishes the ultimate divorce
and simplifies business.
I, myself, believe that force
allows the resolution of conflict.
I also believe in the right to bear arms
and the God-given right to settle scores,
but I did not measure my courage
by the size of my dick,
which I shook always after I peed,
so I would not stain my jockeys,
though people claim I was careless
with my appearance
and kept a dirty apartment—
rolls of toilet paper strewn on the carpet,
along with cigar butts, wads of money
condoms (so what?),
and other stuff too useless to name.
On that same floor, I lay with whores
without touching once,
if they were not clean,
if they had not washed
with hot water and Dial soap
that would not float like Ivory,
but was better for germs.

Imagine. A man stands trial among gentiles,
who regard him as the enemy,
a Jew they think will steal the pennies
off a dead man's eyes:
therefore, no one comes to his rescue.
Promises are broken.
I am not a man made in the image of my protectors,
so what do I get?—zilch.
Yet, I pay my debts, because I am a stand-up guy.
Even so, they song and dance me.
They light a powder keg under my feet,
which I must tell you always gave me trouble—
calluses, corns, bunions, toenails ingrown.
The chiropodist's office was my home away.
I spent a fortune just to be able
to walk without pain.
Still I could handle whatever came my way
and I can say that without a trace of shame.
A man can brag, if a man's aim is good enough.
But where was my glory,
where was my flag for wrapping in
when shots were fired
and the hired man collapsed
before the other hired man,
who once handed him cold cash
for services rendered
after Lee surrendered cherry like a bride?
Dream lover, he says, you are so mean.
I hit him, sure, not hard,
but just enough to make it rough and make him ready.
I am no fucking queer,
but a man, who enjoys the respect of other men.
I bend him over the couch, take out my strap

and whack his ass, then *him* I allow in my bed.
Afterward, I bathe him with these hands.
I lather him and wash him
the way a mother would a child.
My Lee was an adventurous boy.
One night, he even shows up with an MP,
the kind who calls you kike
and expects you to lick his spit-shined boots
and like it. I am as mad as hell at Lee.
He hits me back. First time.
The smile on his face like the day I shot him.
Next weekend, Ferrie the fairy arrives
and I have to put up with *his* craziness.
He brings a rat in a cage, gets drunk,
lets it out, sobers up. No rat.
He claims he's lost the cure for cancer.
I go out and buy another rat
and pretend I've found the other.
He cannot tell the difference.
Peace restored.
We turn to more pressing problems.
"People with an interest are asking
what we do about Lee," he says,
fixing me with what he thinks is a theatening stare.
"In competition, you know, sports, someone wins
and someone is eliminated."
I nod, no more.
"The door," he asks, "is closed on this then?"
"With a bang," I tell him.
When he's gone, I do some calculating.
I have troubles with the IRS.
There are threats to be met with action.
I am a man without regrets, yet, I know this thing

with Lee will not be easy to forget.
By now, he is like a son to me
and I am Abraham with no reprieve,
because unlike God,
men do not have the luxury of mercy.
So Lee becomes the patsy
and we dishonorable men
obey the first rule of self-preservation,
which is to find a fool to take the blame.
When it's him, or me
who needs a complicated explanation?
Another lone gunman has a plan,
but sometimes plans go awry.
He doesn't realize he, too, is a sacrifice,
until he smells his own flesh burning.

A President is taken by surprise
under the wide-open skies of Texas.
The kings of hearts cry,
"Off with Jack O'lantern's head,"
and two long days later,
I fill the chamber of my snub-nosed .38
with a silver bullet.
I am so patient, standing in the basement,
wearing a new shirt, tie, and suit,
old shoes, my favorite hat.
News is what I am going to make.
I will hand out interviews
as if they are doubloons
and replace Kennedy's and Oswald's faces.
When the elevator doors open,
I stride forward like a businessman
going to make the deal of a lifetime,

but all I do is seal my fate in concrete.
I do not even feel the trigger.
I am as numb as Lee is stunned by my betrayal.
The trap sprung at last, he passes into oblivion
and I pass gas from another bad meal
of pastrami and green onions
and the fact that my ass is now
on the griddle being done.
I am afraid my mask will slip
and I will tip the scales of justice
in the direction of the other assassins,
behind the rose-colored glass,
where Oswald and Ruby take the fall
and all the evidence is made to fit the crime,
at least until I've been abandoned by my friends.
Only then, I say, Chief Justice, I am in danger.
I will tell all if you arrange safe passage to D.C.,
but I receive a strange answer.
Can it be the Chief is a master of deception too?
The Chief says, "You do what's best."
My request for sanctuary is denied.
Now I am nothing but cancer cells.
Even my wife, Sheba, wouldn't recognize me.
So she is a dachshund?
She is the only woman good enough for me.
If only we could be together,
but I walk alone down a tunnel of white light,
then come out in a field of sunflowers,
their heads nodding hello, goodbye.
Some old acquaintances
whose names I can't remember
slap my back, then wander off
and I settle into an endless afternoon

without punishment, or reward
until a dark angel
in the guise of an evangelist
from Los Angeles appears
with the sword of justice in one hand
and a video camera in the other.
He offers me the chance to dance
on the graves of the slaves to the official story,
but why bother?
I bow my head over the edge of the precipice,
where the life I lead
lies dead in its own arms,
while the other victims of the resurrection
are stumbling toward an open car.
They are doomed to repeat the past,
but who can prove the truth
really isn't what you make it,
when it's so easy to fake?
Yet, his argument is so convincing that I waver.
I'll cooperate for one small favor, I tell him,
so we negotiate a detour on the road
to reopened files.
Now, on a city street,
paved with fool's gold,
I testify about the abuse of firearms
and the absolute power of lies,
then I take the few glistening coins from my hat
and throw them in the air.
They rise and rise, then fall back
on the eyes of America,
D-O-A inside a cardboard box.

OSWALD INCOGNITO & ASTRAL TRAVELS

I've seen that face before,
staring at me
from the sixth floor
of the School Book Depository.
Is it déjà vu,
or is it the old story
of finally seeing yourself
in someone else's eyes?
Fake eyes, like the one
Sammy Davis Jr. wore
and used to slip into a stranger's glass of booze.
Once it got caught in somebody's throat.
They had to cut him open.
After Sammy washed it in boiling water,
he popped it back in.
He winked at himself in the mirror,
then he disappeared in a flash of gunfire
left over from the last hour of the assassin,
when three shots either narrowed, or widened, a plot,
depending on how you look at it,
not how it happened.
It wasn't easy being two places the same time,
but I managed the rarest of all magic tricks
with the flick of an eyelid,
I split down the middle,
I ran two directions,
but the lesson in this is
I ran in a circle,
came back where I started.

In my palm, a coin
was gleaming like twilight.
I dropped it down the slot
and got a Coke for my trouble.
The bubbles went up my nose.
I closed my eyes,
but that was no defense
against the magnificence of murder.
I admit to losing my perspective.
I couldn't see not only
that I had become ineffective,
but expendable,
so it was natural that the prime directive
would be to eliminate me.
Who could have predicted
that the shooter would be the man,
who kept boys as, uh, roommates,
who carried rolls of toilet paper
wherever he went as a talisman against disaster
sent straight to the bowels
and expelled with a howl of pleasure.
I'm only here to give voice
to what you've been thinking,
but were afraid to say in front of witnesses,
because they, too, could be the enemy
sent to do you in on TV,
which is itself a form of not being seen.
From the time I was a kid, I hid,
you know, in the back of my mind,
where it's cluttered with boxes of old comics,
whose heroes seduce children
into believing that evil and good
can be recognized by a kiss on the lips,

but my Judas pissed in his coffee,
before offering a sip.
It tasted like it always had,
slightly bitter, then sweet.
I knew what it meant
when Jack stepped from the shadows,
yet, I wanted to believe he was rescuing me.
I would take the gun
and in the best cowboy tradition,
go down in a hail of bullets,
In a split second, I imagined my hand
gripping the weapon,
but as I lay in the ambulance,
I understood the significance
of my death by deception.
Since I had only assumed the identity of myself,
it was somebody else who died,
who'd been saved by his unwitting defection from life.
Termination is, after all, a kind
of natural selection for spies.
It implies survival by escape
from the mass suicides of the pack.
Clowns like Jack Ruby move
through a crowd undetected,
but I am unprotected,
even my pubic hair isn't safe from scrutiny.
I'm not there either.
If I'm anywhere, I'm still trapped
in the palace of lies,
where I'm clothed in illusion
and fed confusion with a spoon.
I take the steps downstairs two-at-a-time.
I flip a penny to see if I should go.

Heads! I stay, but in a moment of panic,
I write my name on the wall
beside the Coke machine. OSWALD
in capital letters.
I erase it with spit and my shirttail,
but it keeps reappearing,
each time the letters get larger,
until the "O" is a hole
I can walk through
and when I finally do, it closes around me
like a mouth around the mouth of a rifle.
The question, though,
isn't what's in a name,
but what's in the barrel.
The answer is nothing,
but when I follow the arrow,
I find it pointing straight at me,
huddled beside a window,
as the President rides by unsuspecting,
only his eyes reflecting surprise
at the moment of impact.
Only one of his eyes breaks free of the socket
and is launched like a rocket,
while a man, shining shoes stops to listen,
as "Birth of the Blues" wafts down the alley,
from a club where Sammy is playing
to standing ovations.
"I need a vacation," Sammy thinks,
when a patron drinks the martini,
where the glass eye is hidden
among the olives and pearl onions
like a gunman on a grassy knoll.
Later, with my shoes buffed to a high sheen,

I stroll into the club,
when Sammy gets booed off the stage,
because of a joke he played that backfired.
"Show's over," the manager tells
the assortment of losers and swells,
so Sammy sits down at the bar.
I offer him a Cuban cigar,
then I light up another.
We smoke in silence,
broken only by the shush
of cars through the slush
of November, turning to winter.
"Ain't it a bitch," Sammy says, at last,
pitching ash in his whiskey,
which he drinks anyway.
"They killed the President
and it's like nothing happened."
I nod, I tug at my threadbare shirt,
as if it can protect me
from the infinite cold.
"One more for the road, babe?" he asks.
I say, no, one last toast
to the President, before I go,
then I raise my glass,
open my mouth wide and swallow.

PARTY LINE

The phone rang this morning,
which is strange,
because our phones rarely work.
No, not even mine.
I stood beside it, my hand
suspended above the receiver.
Finally, I told my aide to answer it,
but the ringing stopped when he picked it up.
As soon as he set it back, however,
it began to ring again.
I started counting backward
5, 4, 3, 2. On 1, I said
Esta es una mala noticia?
The voice repeated my question in English.
Is this bad news?
When I didn't respond, he said, *Fidel?*
There was something familiar about his voice
that came out of the past
the way Kirk Douglas comes for Robert Mitchum
in that movie of the same name.
What comes is back pay, I mean payback.
That's how the Americans say it, no?
But what did I owe this voice
and what did I have left to give,
except my life—the truth, maybe,
but what good would it do me, or you, Jack? I said,
because at last I realized who had phoned me
from his private zone of twilight.
Can I speak to Che,

or is this line restricted to former heads of state?
Only silence greeted my laughter,
then he said, *Why don't you let go too*
like the Russians? You might save your ass and space
on the last plane out, after the coup.
Take the advice of someone who knows
how easily a head explodes
when shot at close range.
I fought a war, remember?
The revolution that broke the stranglehold
you corrupt capitalists had around our balls.
We were even starting to grow breasts.
Yes, I saw with my own eyes,
but instead of destroying our resolve,
it gave us the strength to go on.
Can you say the same?
What did your death inspire? What fierce battles
raged in your memory?
Who paid for your death, aside from that,
what did he call himself, patsy,
who wasn't even guilty?
OK, I said it.
I wrote the book on conspiracies.
Wasn't I the victim of dynamite,
jammed in exhaust pipes, poison pills,
the infamous cigars
and a live grenade in a bar of soap?

I turn everything into a question,
because it keeps the curious at bay.
I disarm that way.
Only Celia knew the true Fidel.
The rest is a ruse.

I'll tell you a joke.
You know how to diffuse a bomb?—
you throw yourself on top of it.
Yes, I know you landed on that blond bomb
of a different kind, though just as lethal.
She shared your secrets. She had keys
to doors that should not be opened.
My friend, it is the nature of whores
to seek to reform themselves by using honesty
the way they once used sex.
It too becomes a commodity.
It is the sweetest revenge.
The sinned against use it
to defend their tarnished honor,
even if it destroys them.
Marilyn Monroe saw you and Bobby
for what you were then,
young men propelled
into a dangerous liaison by their appetites,
but you fooled her. You were not controlled by them.
You were merely compromised,
but she was dead. What a price she paid.
Instead of wedding bells,
she got a lonely immortality.
Eventually, you found your own way there.
Perhaps she got what she wanted after all,
but we did not.
I have lived to see a state of anarchy
descend on my allies
because of a lack of faith.
The Soviets call it dissolution,
as if it were an Alka Seltzer tablet,
dropped in a glass of water.

All that waste, all that haste to get a crumb
off the rapidly emptying table
of the United States.
If this is the answer to our problems,
it has come too late.
In 1963, assassins' guns
severed the one tie I had with anyone
I respected in that government of imperialists,
cut down the only man of vision.
You were a man like me.
I kicked the Mafia out of Cuba, United Fruit,
eliminated prostitution, gambling,
raised the literacy rate.
So I clamped down on intellectuals, created strawberries
which had no taste,
bred cows that gave neither milk, nor meat,
had to import enough to eat, and fuel.
A cruel, unenlightened leader would have killed.
I merely imprisoned those who had defied me
and denied the revolution its due.
A true leader can admit he made mistakes
for the greater good.
Fidel is Cuba; Cuba is Fidel.
I will not lie about my ties to the Medellin Cartel.
Selling drugs is not my business,
no matter what they say,
but the CIA knows all about such things.
I needn't tell you that.
Just follow the trail of disinformation back
to the assassination.
A man in my situation
has to be prepared to slow dance with his enemies.
Everything is permissible

in the struggle for liberation, or for domination.
Therefore, black is white is gray.
Today, I may condemn the man who shot my friend,
tomorrow embrace him.
Statesmanship demands the pistol, the whip,
the kiss of betrayal
and the slipperiness of eels.
I became a master of concealment,
because I knew the game was played for ideology.
Even you were only skin,
stretched over the crumbling page of history.
When you understand you are expendable,
you begin to control your destiny,
while other men become its victims.
I admit misgivings.
I may have outlived my usefulness.
Perhaps I should retire to a ranch
and raise llamas and ostriches,
creatures as exotic as I am now.
The thought torments me.
Has the pried-open fist of thirty-odd years
suddenly revealed socialism as another bankrupt ideal,
sealed in the blood of martyrs to the cause?
No, I cannot believe it. No, even to you
from whom out of respect, I hide nothing,
I still say, save socialism.
Socialism, or death.

MIRACLE IN MANILA

A man could never do
as much for Imelda
as a pair of shoes.
I always knew if she had to choose,
it would be pumps instead of passion.
Although her Ferdinand was handy
with his tongue and his fingers,
she preferred to linger
over coffee and a stack of magazines
rather than to have him between her legs.
I could only get the flower
of the Philippines in bed,
when I was dressed in a red jock strap
and tap shoes.
Even then, she might fade
into another rambling monologue,
or nap fitfully,
until I tap-danced and sang, "Feelings,"
a song I hated,
but marriage is a compromise
and many times, I had to sing two choruses,
before she woke and sang along
and with the last ounce of my energy,
I would take off those goddamn shoes
and do my duty as a man.
A woman like Imelda
must be wooed again and again,
because she is controlled by her moods,
which are dark and greedy,

and every day, they chew her up
and spit her out,
less a few clothes and jewels
and more of the slum she came from.
Now she's too old to play the ingenue.
The loyal few won't admit
that she no longer matters.
They grovel at her feet,
while she holds court
in a hotel suite.
Otherwise, she's mostly ignored,
so isolated and bored with herself,
she takes to her beloved stores.
She gives away her shopping bags of evening clothes
to the poor maids,
who have no more use for them than I do,
lying in my refrigerated coffin.
Finally, she has a meeting with Mother B,
who has been crucified every Good Friday
for the last five years.
Between sips of diet soda and tears,
Imelda decides the time is right
for her own brief sojourn on the cross,
so she goes to San Fernando with her entourage.
She wears a simple shift designed in Paris,
and handmade flats.
She even holds the special nails,
soaked in alcohol for a year,
to her nose, and inhales,
before she lets the attendants
drive them into her hands and feet,
just missing bones and blood vessels.
Only a few heartbeats and she is down,

waving to the crowd,
who shout her name,
as if she really is the President.
It's then she starts to bleed
from her palms.
Somebody screams, then they all do.
It seems like hours
before they rush toward her,
tearing at her clothes, her hair,
pleading for cures, for food,
for everything they've ever needed.
Only gunfire drives them back
and she flees, both horrified and pleased
that the trick worked.
Once the fake blood's washed off,
she stares at her hands,
almost wishing she really had stigmata.
She doesn't even make the news.
I mean, they get her confused with Mother B,
who seizes credit for the "miracle."
Imelda lets it go.
She settles for self-mockery
and sings "Memories,"
while her guests dine on Kentucky Fried Chicken,
flown in by Federal Express.
When she's alone, she gets undressed
and lies down,
not even bothering to get beneath the covers.

Next morning, they find her
drained of her blood,
but her heart's still beating
and she suddenly sits up,

repeating my name.
She says in a vision,
I gave her a pair of magic slippers,
that allow her to walk on water.
She's lying, but I'm past caring
and I'm done with shoes.
Anyway, she doesn't need me,
because she's got her illusions.
After a transfusion, a facial,
and a manicure,
she's campaigning again, although it's useless
and I'm back tap-dancing by her side,
while she proclaims herself
the only candidate
who can rise from the dead.

KNOCKOUT

For Desiree Washington and Mike Tyson

So Miss Desiree Washington was a feast
for the sweet beast.
Well, I ain't no good Christian girl.
Ain't nobody gonna give up they seat
on the bus for me.
I don't even get nothing to eat
before they have me up against the wall,
or down on the floor.
Y'all think it's all the same
that we just poor black crackwhores
lay on our asses all day,
then come out at night like vampires
to suck up all your money.
Y'all think we spread our legs
and AIDS comes flying out.
Say we get paid to do it.
Got no right to fight
if y'all men get it into y'all heads
to make us fuck a whole housefulaniggers for free,
then kick us in the teeth,
'cause we gave it up easy,
but y'all folks look at her a different way.
Y'all say she respectable, educated.
Say Tyson shoulda waited
'til he found himself a squeezer like me.
Y'all say nothing shaking there 'cept her hair,
but this where I disagree, see,
'cause it's a fine line
between rape and a good time.

You find that out real fast
when you got an uninvited dick up your ass.
It ain't that far from "Star Search"
to leaning in car windows
asking for more money than you ever gonna get,
even if you shit gold.
This one bitch know what she talking about.
I ain't gonna shut up.
This is my mouth. You ain't paying my rent.
I ain't got no pimp.
I don't need no sonofabitch taking my money.
I let them bill collectors do that.
I got two kids living with my mama.
She trying to take 'em
like she gonna be able to raise 'em by herself.
She says I'm irresponsible,
a whore and a drug addict.
It's just talk. She take my money, don't she?
Then she walk over to the store,
get her some wine and a pack of cigarettes
before she buy them kids a thing to eat.
I seen her do it. But they clean, though.
They got a place to sleep.
I can't say that.
I got evicted last week.
Come home, found all my shit in the street.
Niggers picking through it like it was trash.
Had to almost fight to get my own shit back.
One of my friends out there.
He said, "Rhonda, what you doing back so early?"
And what she doing out with a man
that time of morning,
if she so goody-goody?

I'll tell you what.
She think 'cause she special,
she gonna be safe.
Hell, ain't nobody safe no more.
She walk into the lion's cage,
but she ain't Daniel.
She just another black girl
in a man's world
and she on the bottom getting fucked
just like I am.

FINISHED

You force me to touch
the black, rubber flaps
of the garbage disposal
that is open like a mouth saying, ah.
You tell me it's the last thing I'll feel
before I go numb.
Is it my screaming that finally stops you,
or is it the fear
that even you are too near the edge
of this Niagara to come back from?
You jerk my hand out
and give me just enough room
to stagger around you.
I lean against the refrigerator,
not looking at you, or anything,
just staring at a space which you no longer inhabit,
that you've abandoned completely now
to footsteps receding
to the next feeding station,
where a woman will be eaten alive
after cocktails at five.
The flowers and chocolates, the kisses,
the swings and near misses of new love
will confuse her,
until you start to abuse her,
verbally at first.
As if trying to quench a thirst,
you'll drink her
in small outbursts of rage

then you'll whip out your semiautomatic,
make her undress, or to listen to hours
of radio static as torture
for being amazed that the man of her dreams
is a nightmare, who only seems happy
when he's making her suffer.

The first time you hit me,
I left you, remember?
It was December. An icy rain was falling
and it froze on the roads,
so that driving was unsafe, but not as unsafe
as staying with you.
I ran outside in my nightgown,
while you yelled at me to come back.
When you came after me,
I was locked in the car.
You smashed the window with a crowbar,
but I drove off anyway.
I was back the next day
and we were on the bare mattress,
because you'd ripped up the sheets,
saying you'd teach me a lesson.
You wouldn't speak except
to tell me I needed discipline,
needed training in the fine art
of remaining still
when your fist slammed into my jaw.
You taught me how ropes could be tied
so I'd strangle myself,
how pressure could be applied to old wounds
until I cried for mercy,
until tonight, when those years

of our double exposure end
with shot after shot.

How strange it is to be unafraid.
When the police come,
I'm sitting at the table,
the cup of coffee
that I am unable to drink
as cold as your body.
I shot him, I say, he beat me.
I do not tell them how the emancipation from pain
leaves nothing in its place.

RESPECT, 1967

The porch light isn't even on,
when I come home, ready to fight.
My wife hopes I'll trip on the steps,
crack my head open and bleed to death,
so that when she gets up,
all she has to do is phone the police,
the ambulance, and my mother,
who will agree with her that I had it coming,
coming home all hours, slamming doors,
all the while godamning women and children,
who stand in the way of a man's good time.
You bitches, I yell, as I go
from empty room to occupied,
I decide how much is too much noise,
so get ready, because I'm putting on Aretha Franklin.
She knows what I need,
although what I've got is marriage,
is babies and bills,
instead of chills up the spine
and wine chilled on ice
by a nice piece of ass,
who doesn't talk back.
You sluts are going to take what I'm giving,
whether it's beatings, or dick.
A man is not kneeling for whores.
Open your doors, or I'll kick them in,
or I'll send a whole legion of men,
armed with their rage
against the paycheck that must be saved for diapers

and milk, Tampax
and all the messy stuff that is female,
when us males want silk underwear
to tear off strange women, who don't care
if we're late, if we're impotent, or make requests
for sex, sex, and sex
and let us go spinning like the asteroids we are,
broken off from one planet of responsibility
to ram ourselves into another,
or to burn up in the atmosphere
of the fear that is manhood.

FAMILY PORTRAIT, 1960

"Sutton," my wife says,
"the girls won't wash between their legs."
What am I supposed to do about it? I think,
having just come in
from buying round steak
that I will try to tenderize with a mallet,
then salt and pepper, dredge in flour
and fry
and serve with green peas, biscuits, gravy.
But Stella (Peggy to her friends),
yells from her bed,
"Girls, go in the bathroom
and take off your clothes."
She leans back on her pillow,
a box of Melba toast,
cradled in one arm
like a cardboard teddybear,
a barrier against the poverty and disappointment
which have put her there. Colitis, doctor says.
And where is this?—
one of those apartments
with a courtyard in Los Angeles,
where waitressing in cafe once
she served the guy from TV,
Route 66, that is, coffee,
but now I bring her coffee, bring her cigarettes
and pretend to sympathize,
but now my daughters stand before me,
wearing only shower caps:

Roslynn, seven years,
thin and unpredictable,
and Florence, eleven,
also thin and obedient to a fault.
I hand them washcloths, soap,
and shoo them in the shower.
They stand in the water
and wait for my commands.
"Go on," I say, "you know how to start."
Necks and shoulders, chests, backs and bellies.
Down they go and in between the smooth,
hairless entrances into themselves.
"You call that washing?" I say,
and lean forward on my toes,
bend my knees and spread them.
"See," I say
and use my hand between my own legs,
"like this, get in there,
scrub your little pussies."

After dinner,
Florence washes dishes, Roslynn dries.
Stella watches television,
while I doze
and chaos kept at bay,
lies down to sleep with us
until daylight.

LIFE STORY

For Father Ritter and other priests accused of sexual abuse.

Nuns are the brides of Christ,
but priests are His sons,
sons denied the sexual release
of giving themselves up to the spirit.
Christ is not raped, until he hails Caesar,
no, not Him,
but isn't it logical,
can't we imagine it going that far?
For examined in that context,
the rest snaps into place.
To rape is to erase the other's identity
and replace it with your own,
so why not ram it home, eh,
the Roman way (copied from the Greeks, of course).
Strip Him, whip Him, bend Him over and . . .
Suddenly, I imagine the blond hustler
with the black Georgia O'Keefe crosses
tattooed on his butt cheeks.
Ah, let me count the ways.
But most days, I conduct myself
in a conventional fashion.
I perform my desperate acts only in my thoughts.
I talk to God from one side of my mouth.
I say Mass, pass out the host
and most of the time,
I only drink wine for consolation,
but once in a while,
I raise the black flag of moral surrender
and I get out my visual aids.

My hand trembles, as I turn each page,
where men and boys are displayed like offerings,
their cocks to be seized and squeezed,
until I drown in jizzum,
until I leave my prison
to walk the tightrope
to the next broken boy,
the next indiscretion that could destroy me.
This one's what they used to call consumptive.
"Do you need a place to stay?" I ask.
In bed, he says, he's afraid of the dark,
so I leave the light on.
Toward daylight, I strike.
He says, "Daddy, don't,"
but daddy do and do
and when I'm through,
I give him a few dollars
and a card that says
Need Help? Call 1 (800) 4–Refuge.
But what about my own help line to salvation?
The voice always says,
I'm not in right now, leave a message,
so at the sound of sizzling flesh,
I repeat my request for rescue.
What is it I want to escape?
Are the boys merely substitutes
to save me from some greater abomination?
In my dreams, the centurion has my face,
holds Christ by the waist
and kisses his navel,
sticks his tongue there,
surprised to find the taste
of honey filling his mouth.

The sound of bees also fill his ears,
as he spreads his cloak on the floor
and shoves Christ down on it.
When he feels stinging in his groin,
he finds his pubic hair alive with bees.
His cock swells to an enormous size,
turns black and he dies,
staring into Christ's eyes.
Still He had not spoken,
had seemed to open and open Himself
to the centurion,
only to take His revenge
at the moment of consummation.
Am I going somewhere with this,
or am I only trying to discover who is who
in the locked room of sexual abuse?
One is the picture
and the other is the frame around it.
I found it!—the photograph
of Father Harrigan and me when I am five.
He holds me in his lap.
I'm tired, though I've had my nap.
It's June, I mean he said he had a june bug,
to come to his room to see.
Did I say he is my uncle?
By the time I'm thirteen,
we have so many secrets between us—
my tiny hand, a penis
that I stroke
the way he taught me,
he who bought me my first missal
and who later welcomes me into the seminary.
He teaches me how to capture little boys

with promises of toys,
until a free meal
becomes the lure
with which the fish
are hooked, then filleted
and cooked.
I remember how he shook me,
when I wouldn't touch.
"Do not tease me, boy. Please me," he said,
"or, or . . ."
He shuddered, he jerked away from me
and that was that, until next time.
Finally, I'm at his grave.
When I fall on my knees, father pulls me up.
"I know everything," he whispers, "I know.
When we get home, you pack. You leave."
When he has his final heart attack,
I sit with his body for hours.
I think some power to change
may drain from him to me,
but I feel nothing
brushing against my soul,
except the old urge.

After the funeral,
mother and I find letters from my uncle
in a tattered, old suitcase.
Before I can stop her, she opens them.
She smothers a cry
when she comes to the photograph of me
in the buff, a dust broom
stuck up my anus.
I stare at it, amazed I had forgotten it happened.

Uncle begs forgiveness, in each letter,
but father never forgives.
The last, dated the year before he died
is five pages (the shortest).
Again he describes how he robbed me of my innocence,
but says I can at least do good as a priest.
Twice mother tries to speak.
At last, she says, "You were always such a sweet boy."
She rips the letters up
and throws them in the trash.
"And give me that," she cries.
Finally, the photograph in shreds, she opens her hands
in a gesture of helplessness,
then says, "I'll fix you supper."

Later, we embrace and I go outside.
I spread my arms around the ancient oak,
where uncle tied me once,
until I took him inside my mouth.
I thought my throat would close,
but instead it froze open,
while snow and semen
spilled down into me.
I was ten and I was praying to die,
praying I would choke,
while he commanded me to open wider.
Finally, I couldn't breathe.
I passed out and when I came 'round,
my mouth tasted of soap.
Uncle spoke, "Lie on your side."
I felt him poking me with something,
then I felt myself pried apart,
as I began to lose consciousness again.

"Still friends?" he asked next time.
"What are you drawing?"
It was a flying man, his head
severed from his body
and falling to earth,
but I said, "It's the Holy Ghost."
"No," he said, "this is your uncle,
this is the end of hope."
He hung himself with rope.
We priests did our best to hide it,
pretended not to know the truth,
though the proof was in his room.
One filthy magazine after another
and nude photos, scattered on the bed and floor
were there for unavoidable discovery.
They delegated me the burning
of the evidence,
the lies about the whys of his closed casket.
We found a way around it all,
got him into hallowed ground.
An accident, a fall, we told everyone.
Hit his head, bled profusely,
found dead hours later . . .
I slammed his head against the radiator,
then notified the police.
We came to an agreement
for the good of the Church.
They would not release the report.
We could sort it out ourselves, couldn't we?

I throw my duffle in the car
and back out of the drive.
When the hustler I pick up

moves across the seat,
I feel no beast rising beneath his hand.
"Go on, get out," I say
"and stay away from creeps like me."
"I'll see you again," he says, because he knows.
I know he will too, unless I lose my head some afternoon
and like a June bride, marry groom death.
At the next intersection,
I head west, instead of south.
Along the way, I shed my priesthood
like a skin.
I work my way from one end
of decline to another.
Sometimes I drink for days,
then take any job that pays enough
for sandwiches.
After two thousand miles, I sell the car
and tend bar in Wickenburg,
until a memory disturbs my false serenity.
Twin boys, who lived on our street,
forced to eat off the floor,
while uncle bored into them
with a vibrator.
Later, he showed a video of Peter Pan,
which was written by a man
not too different from me,
for as I understand it,
Captain Hook may be taken
as the unexpressed desire
to molest a child, to threaten him with harm,
then ultimately to defile him.
Now when people stare at the stub
where my hand was, I smile and rub it,

as if a genie will appear
and grant three wishes.
I am that which I fear.
Is that why you cleared out, uncle dear,
though here you are in a puff of smoke,
the scar of your life healed over now.
How much farther must I go?
Why is my destination so uncertain?
What is the difference between nothing and zero?
Cackling, you fade to black
and I'm staring through the bars
at LA County, where I am incarcerated
for another sex-related incident
that escalated into violence.
He participated willingly I told them,
as the boy was hustled off
to join the war against the saints,
who aren't just the good ones, no,
but also the ones who struggle again and again
against the flow of raw sewage,
only to drown in its undertow.

THE ICE CREAM MAN
National Ice Cream Day, 1991

You know what I've got
in my white van besides popsicles,
Eskimo pies, and ice cream sandwiches?
Little girl, I've got video cameras, props,
cans of whipped cream for hot fudge sundaes
that are not for eating, but for teasing
the camera and the man behind it.
Come on in, Sherry.
Suck a pop-up for Jerry.
Get it way down your throat. You won't choke.
Old Jerry won't let you. Let me get you another.
Your mother won't mind.
How 'bout if I give you this shiny new dime?
Abracadabra! See? It's yours,
if you give me something too.
Fair's fair, right?
And if the boogie man comes tonight,
you can give it to him to leave you alone,
or better yet, tomorrow,
when mommy and daddy aren't home,
call old Jer' on the phone. No, better not.
OK, honey, now how 'bout we play
the mommy and daddy game? Let's see.
What's Jerry got in his dress-up box? Whoa.
A feather boa, green to go
with those green eyes,
bright red lipstick for my piggy wiggy.
Surprise! Look what I found,
a gown just like mommy wears

on nights when daddy's head's down
where it shouldn't be.
Oh, I see them all right.
My mommy and Stan, my brand-new daddy,
who puts his hand down my pants,
when mommy isn't there.
He wears a torn tee shirt and no undies
and neither does mommy,
as they roll on the floor
and I can't get away before she sees me
and he does
and she says, "Come here, Gerald dear,"
but I won't go near. I'm afraid.
I start to cry, but she gets up
and squeezes me against her.
She's so smelly and sticky and I can't breathe.
It's so icky.
Then she says, "Kiss me
and give Daddy Stan a kiss, too,"
and what's he doing to my wee-wee?
Sherry, Sher, open your legs for Jer.
That's right. Smile for the camera and Jerry
and for mommy and Stan on his knees
with his mouth open
and his sharp yellow teeth that bite
until I bleed.
Smile for me, honey,
or better yet, just say, "freeze."

ARCHANGEL

For Chet Baker

You stepped through
the Van Gogh blue curtain
into my dream.
That day in Paris,
we sat at the outdoor café for hours.
I had high breasts
and my dress was cut low.
You leaned close to me, so close;
yet, did not touch.
"I don't need to," you said, "it's the dope,
it's the rush
so much better than lust.
Hush, take a deep breath
and you'll just go to sleep like I did."
I knew you were hustling me,
that underneath the hipster philosophy
lay the same old Chet out to score.
Still, I lent you money, still I followed you
to the pissoir,
where Lucien gave you "le fix."
Shaking his head, he pocketed the money and said,
"I heard you were dead,"
and you answered, "I am."
You said when you slammed into the pavement,
Amsterdam shook, then settled back into apathy,
the way we all do, when we are through
with the foolishness of living.
You ended up sharing your works with a whore
who waited outside the pissoir door,

your generosity as pathetic
as it was predictable.
You wanted sainthood like everybody else.
Instead, you earned the wings
that were too late to save you,
but not too late to raise you
up to junkie heaven.
Later, we stood on the steps of Notre Dame.
You were calm, as you pointed to the bell tower.
You said you saw Quasimodo up there,
holding Esmeralda over the edge
by her hair,
but all I saw staring down were the gargoyles
who'd found peace,
because it meant nothing to them.
"I see," I lied, to please you,
but you knew and you blew me a kiss.
You wished me "bonne chance,"
then you eased into flight,
as the cool, jazzy, starry night
opened its arms to retrieve you.

LUST, LOVE, AND LOSS

1 ZERO VELOCITY, I

Leave your porkpie hat on, lover,
the one you bought in that vintage clothing store.
Do it for mother, do it for your little whore.
What poor excuses for passion we use
to get the juices going
now that we've been together four years.
You say, "Please don't do it,"
but you know it will arouse me,
because begging is all that's left to unfreeze me.
I tear your black tee shirt off you.
I try to bite through your underwear too,
but you stop me when my teeth
get caught in your pubic hair,
tangled and damp, reddish brown and wiry,
so different from the hair on your head,
which is fine and straight.
You make me wait as you slip the black bikinis
below your hips
and I take the tip of your cock in my mouth,
then let it slip out as you back up and move forward
making your own rhythm,
taking me the way you always do.
When you yell and jerk against my mouth,
come splashes my chest
and you rub it into my skin,
as if marking me somehow,
but it's too late,

though once we were in whatever this is together.
"You shouldn't ever have to defend yourself
for loving," you say,
but every time we fuck, you ask too much of me.
You want ecstasy
when all there is is apology.
"I came too fast," you say, "forgive me."
Forgive you? I ask. Forgive you?
I take the side by the window, you by the door.
You begin to snore and mumble in your sleep.
I keep telling myself that suffering just for love,
or want of it
only counts in literature,
until you slide your hand between my thighs.
Your eyes are closed, but you are awake.
Your rough as a cat's tongue rakes my nipples.
O baby, you murmur,
are you ready for your popsicle?
Everything seems wet; even the walls are sweating,
as we grind and groan down the road
we've been traveling
since the afternoon when I picked you up hitchhiking.
Heading east? I asked.
"Anyplace but here," you said.
I told you that was the title of a novel
and you said you didn't read,
you watched TV and peed outside when you could.
I knew we would fuck,
because you were so different from me
and I needed that then,
but I didn't expect the eternity of true lust
to keep holding on to me.
Let me go, I moan,

but you just go on, until the spasms subside
and I feel like I'm up above my body looking down,
as our breath slows, our hearts,
everything, until it starts all over
like the motor, when I turned the key
and we shot forward
at such high speed
no one could even see us.

Whatever it is, you want it.
You want to buy
the tomato-red '55 Cadillac convertible
and just drive,
maybe with me beside you, maybe not.
You want to bite into my heart's green apple,
and more than that,
if you can get it and you can
from me, or any other woman.
You want to blow this town,
without goodbyes, regrets,
but when the car finally stops
at the edge, it's I, not you, who jump,
I, who leave you standing
in your cutoffs and GAP tee shirt,
my eyes closed, until the sound of spinning wheels,
until you fall through the air beside me,
just pass me and crash
and climb from the wreck
and ask whether it was as good for me
as it was for you?
But I don't answer, because I'm forty-two,
because I'm crashing into the cliché
you just erected between us.
Then I have my hands around your penis
and here among the glass and twisted metal,
the trash tossed out the window
of my last affair,
we try to scare ourselves into each other. We try.
We always say it's the other one's fault,
it's the memory of salt from some other wound

that burns us until we swoon
into the arms of a stranger,
the danger passed out like a drunk in a doorway,
until next time.
You pretend it doesn't matter and so do I,
though unlike you, I know it's only jaded innocence
that keeps me cruising passion's strip
for someone. "Anyone," I whisper,
as you lift my pelvis to your mouth,
your tongue, your pale skin one blur
against the blue blur of the sky.

The bus was full the rainy afternoon
we sat across the aisle from one another
and unashamed, I stared at you.
You had a choirboy's face,
tempered by the promise of sin.
I thought you were a pretty man,
the kind who was too dangerous
for anything but friendship.
When I got off, I was surprised
to find you matching my stride
through the pools of standing water.
One block, two blocks,
upstairs to my apartment.
I still remember the slow, sweet time
before the foreplay ended.
We never spoke.
We kept our separate war and peace to ourselves,
until one day, you broke the spell.
"I'm James," you said,
and I told you the intimacy of names
was still too much to ask of me,
but you insisted,
and we lost the game of keeping things simple
and plain as a Shaker hatbox,
where we could store our past
poor failures at loving.
I don't want to see you anymore, I said, one day
as you were leaving,
but suddenly, I wanted to suck your fingertips
and twist those long strands of your hair
in my hands until you begged me

to make love to you again,
so I pulled you back inside.
I wish the floor had opened up and swallowed me,
but here we are five years from then,
locked in our wedded misery.
Sex without responsibility
could have saved us from disaster,
but now it's too late,
now love's a letter stamped "return to sender,"
stamped "surrender" on delivery.

The blond man with high cheekbones
sent a shiver down my spine.
I knew he was mine
before we'd even spoken
and finally, when he broke through
the emptiness between us,
I sat above him and drove myself
down on his penis,
ground myself against him.
We kissed, until he bit my lip
and I accepted love in all its brutality and sweetness.
"My dove," I whispered, "my life to be,
to sleep beside and hold
against an eternity of loneliness."
But suddenly, I woke in the old brass bed.
My cats slept peacefully
curled against my legs and side.
I tasted blood,
as morning arrived, wearing its disguise of sunlight.

RECONCILIATION

1 BIRTH MOTHER

I wasn't wearing anything but my underwear
when the social worker opened the orphanage door.
I was only four months along
and I didn't show much.
I'd gone out the back
when your father'd come at me with a crowbar.
I'd been sitting on the bed,
painting my toenails the pearl pink he liked,
when he got too quiet.
It had doom in it, that quiet of his.
When he swung at me, I heard him say,
"Goddamn, I bit my tongue,"
but I was running so fast I got past him
and all he got was my slip,
when he grabbed at me.
I thought of staying, of taking the old knife
I used to slice hunks of roast beef
for him to eat Sunday dinner
and cutting him up
just like I'd do that meat for him,
before he'd even eat it
like he was a child, or something, not a man.
All he knew was giving pain and pleasure
and I knew I ought to leave,
but when I measured him against the others,
I only wanted him more.
Every time I swore I was through with him.

I was a blue and black bruise
without the will to choose another way of living,
until I knew that you were coming, son.
Born for no one and no one caring
whether you were dark haired and fair like your mother,
or had your father's olive skin,
brown hair, and hazel eyes.
You had nothing to lose,
so I left you at the orphanage,
when you were born.

After I went back to him,
he'd kid me about that night.
He called it the Friday night fight
and said they should have put it on TV,
then one day, he keeled over and died
in the middle of cursing me,
just like in a fantasy I'd had once. It was the best,
the sweetest revenge.
I packed up. I moved again.
The roads I traveled
with no end to them
and you were back there somewhere,
before it really fell apart for me,
before I couldn't go back,
even if I wanted to. But I did go back. At last,
and finally, I caught up with you
in some wild bar, among the white trash,
who were your kin, beneath your southern gentleman clothes.
Glasses of booze were lined up
on the bar in front of you
and your head was down in your hands
and when I came to stand beside you,

you raised your face and stared at me and turned away.
I knew those eyes
and I hated you. Inside my love was a hate
as fierce as it had ever been for him.
That's when I swung at you with my fist
and hit with all my strength
and didn't miss.

2 OEDIPUS, THE SON

When I was young,
I'd just pick up and go
when I got restless,
but now I know
all my runaways lead
to my adoptive mother,
to the backyard when I'm sixteen
and she slaps me hard,
when I tell her my drinking and dad's is her fault.
At the private schools
I'm always politely asked to leave,
everybody always says I only need another chance
and I always get it,
that is, until now at thirty-six,
when all I see glaring at me from the mirror
of my past is wasted time
and my mother's hand against my fly.
I'm too surprised to move, or even breathe,
until she squeezes me there.
I fall to my knees,
then onto my side, curled in a ball.
Even when the pain has eased,
I lie staring at the maple trees,
whose green leaves are turning gold.
Finally, I'm numb in a way that makes me whole,
makes me her son,
because she'd goaded me into it at last
and now that I am,
she wants to tear me to pieces
like those rags she uses
to wipe my dad's spilled drinks from the floor.

Later, while dad's passed out in the den,
I go into the bedroom.
The sheet only covers my mother's thighs.
The bra she wears is transparent
and her nipples are quarter-sized.
I walk to the bed,
she lifts her head, smiles and lies back,
when I sit down.
Soon, I find her mouth with mine.
At first, she's too tight to enter,
but eventually, she loosens for me
and when she cries, I press harder and deeper.
Afterward, we lie gasping and trembling,
until we sleep.
When I wake and dress,
I find my suitcase in the hall.
At the front door, she calls,
but I don't answer,
I walk outside
and turn down the walkway toward town.
I hear nothing but the sound of my own footsteps,
striking the pavement
and I imagine it is her flesh I am walking on
and that flesh collapsing into bone
under my weight.
At the crossroads, no sphinx greets me
with a riddle to link me to anything wrong
or out of the natural order of things.
One bird begins to sing, another,
the sky is lightening
and only now that I've come back again
to nurse her in my fashion,
now that she is old

and pretending to have forgotten everything,
I realize I did not violate the laws of the gods
which dictate our lives by destroying them
and by calling it fate,
but by taking my mother's body
not out of love, or even hate,
but merely out of self-defense.

3 MOTHERHOOD

When you caught me with my lover, son,
I wasn't ashamed.
I was glad to initiate you into my games of deception.
Though you were sixteen,
to me you were still the three-year-old
from the Irish Hill Orphanage,
crying as you held the dime
your birth mother'd left you out to me,
when I'd come to take you home.
You ought to know that love cannot be bought,
or sold, only taken,
when it's thrown at your feet
like a bone, the bit of meat still on it,
not enough to satisfy,
but just enough to make your hungrier,
to make you cry, until you've eaten
yourself alive, or dead.
That's all love is you know.
It's just a cry that goes unanswered,
a body on top of another body,
pretending to be something more.
Love is your mother
who slams the door in the face of her lover
at 4 PM on Saturdays
when your father is passed out again,
his latest bout of drinking dry martinis
over for the weekend.
His Sunday recovery, when he wakes
begins at noon
with steaks and new potatoes which he cannot eat,
but cooks for us,

as if performing some kind of penance
for the life sentence we call a family.
As always he breaks down, apologizes.
I stare at my plate, until he makes me look at him,
by yelling at me that it's my fault he drinks
and that you do,
then he screams go on, get out,
but we lift our forks, our knives.
We cut our meat,
until today when your seat is empty.
I find you in the yard,
the hard glare of the July sun
shining off the dime now hung
from the chain around your neck.
The table's set, come in, I say,
but you tell me I'm a whore
like your real mother. All women are.
I slap you across the mouth,
though what I want to do is inhale
the incense of whiskey I'll find there,
until I am drunk too
and free of myself like you and your father
pretend to be
just by swallowing your poison.
You think your will's as strong as mine,
but I'll take you to the edge and pull you back.
Only mother love can save you, son,
in a way that can't be measured, or understood.
It is a charm that only mothers possess,
even foster ones,
a spell that won't let go of you
until you give in, or are destroyed.
Men call it emasculation,

but women know it's simply a different kind
of penetration
much like our own when we are plowed and sown
by men who leave the waste
of their ejaculation inside us.
When I lay my hand against your fly
and squeeze you until it hurts,
I feel I can go on living.
I will not die forgiven for my sins
and later, when you sneak into my room,
we do not speak, but seek each other's emptiness,
as if we could ever fill ourselves.
Your lips, my tongue, we are one body.
While your father lies awake
in the next room,
we make our love out of our hatred,
then we sleep
and when we wake, I've packed your suitcase
and like your birth mother, one minute you are here,
then you are gone,
but that was all so long ago
and you've come back to nurse me
now that unlike Jocasta I know the only punishment
to fit my crime is forgetting it.
I'm going blind,
my eyes plucked out by time and not my fingers.
All our attempted suicides have failed forever.
We will never tear ourselves apart
from the afternoon that started this.
I *am* your mother, son
and it is awful. It is bliss.

The smell of formaldehyde fills the car,
as your mother sleeps fitfully beside me.
In my mind, I rehearse our deceit.
The thing was better off, better gotten rid of,
so the deed was done
and everyone is safe from scandal:
You, son, me, your mother and her lover.
Although it wasn't mine, I paid for it to leave,
so it belongs to me
as surely as if it had spurted from me,
during one of your mother's and my rare couplings,
had clung to her uterine wall,
before being thrust out in a rush of air.
Now it's back there in the trunk,
a chunk of discarded meat,
floating in its sweet preservative.
Five hundred miles to Chicago to do it discreetly
and five hundred back.
At first, she lay cramped in the backseat,
but that was before we argued
about stopping at a motel.
She didn't want to,
she wanted only to go, go, until the trip was over
and she could slip back into her infidelities.
Once she'd healed, it would begin again.
I accepted that. Still I wanted some sign from her
to tell me that I mattered.
She sits on two pillows,
her head rolling this way and that,
sits as far apart from me as she can,
as the sky grows blacker and blacker.

They call this tornado weather.
I press my foot hard on the pedal,
then release it slowly,
because beneath it all I'm a coward.
I feel the bottle of bourbon, cradled between my legs,
its hard, cool, reassuring glass asking nothing of me,
only giving what I want and no more.
Your mother is not a whore, son,
nor any one of the poor names
that people call a woman of her kind.
It will serve, I guess, but if pressed, I'd have to choose
a less excusing word.
She uses men to do her bidding; therefore she is a queen
and her queendom is called
the art of seduction and control.
She holds men under her still waters,
until they start to drown in her rejection.
Those who revive always decide
she did not mean to do it.
That's how you get through it, son, you run
not away from her, but back into her arms,
crossed over her chest Egyptian style,
even when she lets you get close enough
to clean up her latest mess.
"Just an indiscretion," she said
two months after you left.
I pretended not to hear,
until my thirst for lies
made me look into her eyes,
red and swollen from crying
tears that meant nothing,
but I seized them anyway
like prizes won after a long struggle.

"I'm so glad I'm the one you turned to," I said,
"I'll help you through. You are my wife."
She said, "My life is ruined."
She never mentioned me, or you.
Until today, I didn't realize what I would do.
While she was with the doctor,
I gave his nurse two hundred dollars and in return
I got the proof of this last affair,
pickled in its juice like I am.

At home, I turn the covers down and carry her to bed.
After I'm sure she is asleep again,
I go to the garage and get a shovel
and in the backyard,
I pick a spot and start to dig.
The small, sealed jar could hold beets,
or even raspberry preserves
some grandmother stirred over a hot flame for hours
and not this nameless thing I'm burying
so deep in my heart no one but her can ever find it
and she will never try.
I pat the dirt down with my hands.
I'll leave her this time, I think. I will,
but when I stand up,
a tornado, shaped like a fetus,
smashes my resolve, before I can escape.

Penis Envy

My wife deserved to be shot.
I served time in the Gulf,
and I am telling you
when I came home and found her packed up and gone,
it wasn't long until I hatched a plan.
I located the man behind it all,
staked out his apartment and his job.
Then one afternoon, I dressed up in camouflage,
loaded my AK-47
and went to Hot Dog Heaven.
I found them in the parking lot,
sharing kisses over lunch.
I came up from behind, but changed my mind
and walked right in front,
and aimed through the windshield,
before they had a chance to see who it was.
I shouted my name, hoping she would hear as she died,
then I went to the passenger side
and fired at his head. A red mass
exploded like a sunburst.
At first, I couldn't believe I'd done it,
then I put the gun down
and looked at my hands, which were steady.
I pulled open the door,
before I knew what I was doing.
I just had to see what he was hiding in his pants.
It was pathetic, a sad, shriveled thing
there between his legs
and not the foot-long

she had said made her scream with pleasure.
I did hear screams, but they were coming
from my mouth, not hers.
Noise, I thought, as I fired at her body again.
Of course, I'd turned the gun on myself.
What else could I do to erase it all?—
the 911 calls, the sirens in the distance,
but the ordinariness of murder overwhelmed me,
possessed me like a spirit
and I thought how easy it would be
to take two or three more people with me.
Instead, I decided to give myself up,
plus I was out of ammunition.
I guess it is my destiny,
to be a living example for other men,
who are only bluffing when they threaten violence.
Now once a week, I write a column on relationships
for the prison publication.
I base my advice on actual situations.
For example, Clarence Thomas.
He had a dick fixation, just as I did.
For me, it was a torment and my downfall
and nearly his.
Ultimately, the question is always
how far are you willing to go?
I think within his perimeters,
Clarence went the distance.
As far as I'm concerned,
he's earned his place on the Supreme Court
and stands tall beside all the other men,
who haven't given in to a woman's scorn,
who are born again from the fire of their ridicule.
If you ask me, Anita Hill got off too easily.

I would have caught the bitch
some afternoon, while the cherry blossoms
were in bloom
and boom, solved all my problems.
Oops! I think I wobbled over the line
that separates fantasy from crime.
The counselors tell me all the time
I've got to get it straight
how the imagination sometimes
races on without us.
But I know Debby and Ed are off somewhere
eating wedding cake
and letting me take the fall for their betrayal.
Is it fair that on the other side of this wall
Clarence has it all
and I have nothing but a ball and chain?
That reminds me, I checked this Othello play
out of the library.
It's about a guy
who loses his reputation and his wife,
well, he kills her, but she made him.
I found some parallels to my own life and Clarence's.
Othello's black.
But the other subtler thing is how a man
must stand up to humiliation,
must retaliate, or lose himself,
who when he finds some pubic hair
in his can of Coke
must ask, regardless of the consequences,
who put it there?

GREED

I was named after my daddy, Vern,
but I was like my mama,
though I'd never admit it, until now.
Before she settled down,
she traveled from town to town
on the roller derby circuit
for the Texas Tornadoes.
Sometimes I went with her.
She always knew how to make me happy.
She'd take me to the nearest hot dog stand
and tell the man,
"Give Verna the works."
She was a big-boned farm girl with flame-red hair
and with the smallest, most delicate feet.
She had to have her skates made specially
and even then, she had to fill them in
with wads of cotton.
I looked like her, but I had daddy's feet,
wide, flat, and reliable.
I wore cowboy boots, a cowboy hat and jeans,
and I was high school rodeo queen of '75.
I learned to drive a tractor, brand cattle
and spit, after I took a bit of chaw.
The boys admired me and asked me out,
but I didn't trust them. They talked too much,
but Russ, the Viet Nam vet,
who drove the school bus was fine for me,
though all in all I'd have to say I wasn't half the girl
I could have been.

A wild mother sometimes makes a cautious child,
who takes the safest path to her destination.
In my case, it was a savings and loan bank,
where at nineteen, I sank
into the routine of being secretary
to Mr. Joe Bob Merriweather,
the president and decent, churchgoing family man.

My change of life began in '82,
when money started pouring in here
like heavy rain through a leaky roof.
All we had to do was set out buckets anyplace
and we would catch a mess of money.
I was polishing my nails lunch time one day,
when a man sailed in the door
and asked me for a date.
Just then, Joe Bob came out
and without a glance at me said, "Boy, she's taken."
After that, we were making love
at least three times a week,
sometimes across the desk
or in the backseat of his Pontiac.
He wasn't that good at it,
but he tried and I was grateful
just to be at his side,
when all his deals paid off.
Then he bought a Rolls.
He partied with politicians and whores,
until word got back to his wife
and she threatened to slit off a piece
of you know what.
After that, he thought he'd better quit it with me too,
so he bought me a sable coat from SAKS JANDEL.

He wished me well
and I sat at my desk, reading the *Wall Street Journal*.
I dabbled in real estate with my latest raise.
I was making one hundred thousand dollars a year,
plus monthly bonus,
and Joe Bob was clearing millions,
building condos, financed through his S & L,
his own contractors, and just plain old-fashioned kickbacks.
We were riding the crest of deregulations wave.
The S & L was like a building without foundation.
How could it stand
longer than a man's imagination?
We were drowning in the illusion of money.
We couldn't be saved.
But that was later.
For a while, I slaved for him,
but then I thought I'd work for my own benefit.
I told mama how he'd used me like I was a slut
he could tip when he got done.
All she said was, "You're just like me.
I could skate all right,
but I couldn't pick men worth a damn.
Your father's a fine example.
You have the brains, the looks.
What took you so long to get what you want?"
I told Joe Bob I'd tell his wife about us.
I said, "Pleading won't get you anywhere.
You're a betting man.
Take out the cards
and deal this hand."
When I went in my own office at last, I cried,
then poured a glass of champagne,
opened a box of Godiva chocolates,
and put my feet up on the desk.

The rest of the time, I learned the trade.
I stayed out of Joe Bob's way and he out of mine.
In time, I had my clients too, a few deals
that added up to two million dollars
in my personal account,
but you know, it didn't amount to much
without love,
which I didn't know was coming
in the form of Bubba Taylor.
Yes, love and hate were waiting in his arms.
He was a charming scoundrel,
who found a way to get my money
that was just setting like a laying hen on eggs.
When he got between my legs,
I was begging for destruction
and it came a mere six months to the day
after I met him.
He robbed me is what he did.
I admit I gave him access to my accounts.
He was my fiancé, wasn't he?
He disappeared just like he'd come
and I had to start over,
only now the government was cracking down
on what it once had ballyhooed
as the way to turn around the banking industry
and free it from the controls
it had enacted in the first place.
Ronald Reagan and his bunch threw out the rules,
but did not go down on the ship of fools,
when it foundered. We did
and we took a lot of people with us.
The unsold real estate piled up—
apartment buildings, condos, homes, and office towers.
Loans in default.

We ought to have known it couldn't last,
but we were past all reasoning.
We had to keep the money moving back and forth
to cover up the fact
that Santa Claus's sack was empty.

Joe Bob took off for parts unknown
and I went home to Abilene,
but not for long.
I was called back to Dallas to testify.
Joe Bob was tried and sentenced to twenty-five years
minimum security, reduced to three,
and when I finished my spiral down
the chain of lies,
I took up keeping books
at Clem's West Side Auto Supply.
They claim the S & L's are getting bailed out,
though it sounds like some of the same shenanigans
are going on at RTC.
They're moving money into other bottomless pockets,
behind the screen of fixing things.
The whole country's on the edge of insolvency,
but I am watching from the sidelines now
like a drunk who's pledged to stay off the bottle,
but the ledge where I'm standing is so narrow.
I could fall back in the fire,
where the money's burning like desire,
only with much more intensity.
Finally, mama and me moved to Vegas,
where I cocktail-waitress at the Sands
and each paycheck I tell the man
at the craps table,
let it ride, until it hurts.